Gearhead Garage

HYDROPLANES

JODIE MANGOR

WORLD BOOK

This World Book edition of *Hydroplanes*
is published by agreement between
Black Rabbit Books and World Book, Inc.
© 2018 Black Rabbit Books,
2140 Howard Dr. West,
North Mankato, MN 56003 U.S.A.
World Book, Inc.,
180 North LaSalle St., Suite 900,
Chicago, IL 60601 U.S.A.

Jennifer Besel, editor; Grant Gould, interior designer; Michael Sellner,
cover designer; Omay Ayres, photo researcher

Library of Congress Control Number: 2016049970

ISBN: 978-0-7166-9305-5

Printed in the United States at CG Book Printers,
North Mankato, Minnesota, 56003. 3/17

CONTENTS

CHAPTER 1

Fast and Fun

The hydroplane roars to life. The engine screams as the boat speeds across the water. A wall of water sprays behind it. It passes another boat as it turns the corner. The race is on!

Rooster Tails

Hydros spray out walls of water called rooster tails.

They can be 60 feet (18 meters) tall.

These tails can be 300 feet (91 meters) long.

Full Speed Ahead

Hydroplanes are some of the fastest **powerboats** in the world. They race on water at top speeds. They can go more than 200 miles (322 kilometers) per hour.

CHAPTER 2

The History of Hydroplanes

Powerboats were invented more than 100 years ago. Drivers quickly learned air slows a boat less than water. The first hydros had angled cutouts in their **hulls**. These "steps" raised the boats' bottoms out of the water.

COWLING

PROPELLER

HULL

COCKPIT

SPONSON

Getting Faster

Early hydros had motorcycle engines. But people wanted faster boats. By the late 1920s, some were using car engines. Then in the 1940s, hydros began using aircraft engines.

COMPARING **TOP SPEEDS** of Hydroplane Classes

Grand National

Limited E

Grand Prix

155.718 miles
(250.6 km)

124.551 miles
(200.4 km)

170.62 miles
(274.6 km)

110.535 miles
(177.9 km)

per hour

317.58 miles
(511 km)

Limited S

Unlimited

(AS OF MAY 2016)

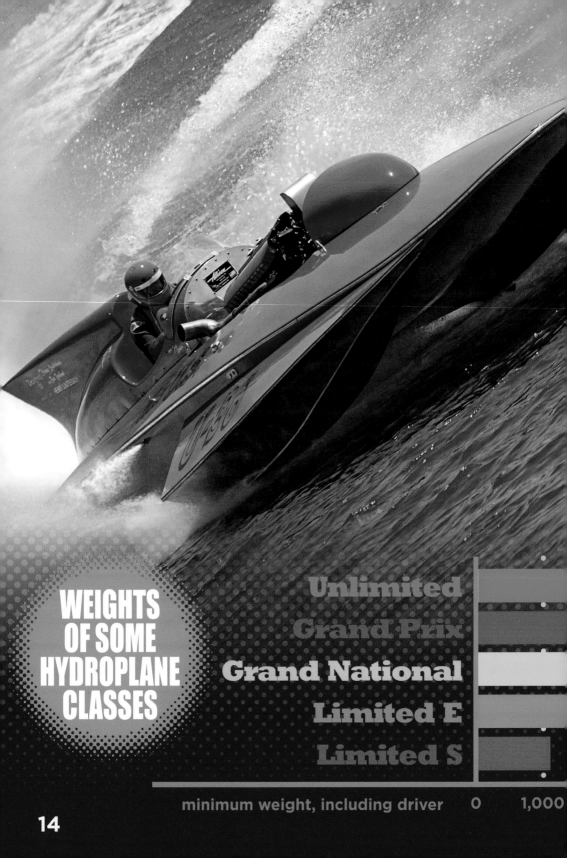

WEIGHTS OF SOME HYDROPLANE CLASSES

Unlimited

Grand Prix

Grand National

Limited E

Limited S

minimum weight, including driver   0   1,000

Hydro Classes

Today, drivers race many types of hydroplanes. Hydro classes are based on engines and weight. Each class has its own rules for racing.

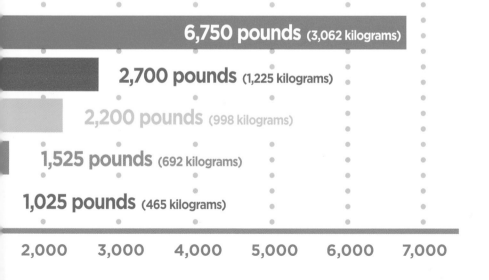

6,750 pounds (3,062 kilograms)

2,700 pounds (1,225 kilograms)

2,200 pounds (998 kilograms)

1,525 pounds (692 kilograms)

1,025 pounds (465 kilograms)

2,000   3,000   4,000   5,000   6,000   7,000

30 feet (9 m)

Lanes are about 30 feet (9 m) wide.

A RACE CAN BE 3 TO 5 LAPS.

Buoys mark the course.

Courses are
1 to 2.5 MILES
(2 to 4 km)
long.

CHAPTER 3

Built for Speed

The fastest hydros are in the unlimited class. Their engines have about 3,000 **horsepower**. They come from military helicopters.

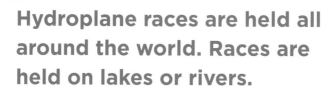

Hydroplane races are held all around the world. Races are held on lakes or rivers.

Fast and Dangerous

Today's hydroplanes are faster than ever. They have very little **drag**. Only three points of the boats touch water. That means the boats ride mostly on air.

Hydroplanes can reach dangerous speeds. They can flip over or crash.

Unlimited hydros have about 27 times more power than cars.

By the Numbers

Hydroplane parts can be very expensive.

ENGINE

AT LEAST **$150,000**

TRAILER **$50,000**

GEARS AND STEERING

ABOUT **$100,000**

CHAPTER 4

The Future of Hydroplanes

Hydroplane racing is an exciting sport. But it also costs a lot. The number of racers has been shrinking. Technology will play a big role in future hydroplanes. Maybe racers will find ways to make these boats less expensive.

Speeding Up

Hydroplane racers and fans love the sport. GPS units are now in hydros to track their speeds. Officials use the data to make races more exciting. The future of hydroplane racing is speeding up!

Safety Features

helmet

safety
cockpit

harness

1978

Hydroplane world speed record is set at 317.58 miles (511 km) per hour.

1945

A new propeller blade is designed. This design is still used today.

1936

The first hydroplane races with a three-point design.

1935

World War II ends.

1945

The first people walk on the moon.

1969

1987

New rules require unlimited hydroplanes to have safety cockpits.

2004

Miss Budweiser, a series of hydros, has its last race. Hydros with this name raced for 42 years.

2016

The Mount St. Helens volcano erupts.

1980

Terrorists attack the World Trade Center and Pentagon.

2001

buoy (BOO-ee)—an object that floats on water to show areas that are safe or dangerous for boats

cowling (KOW-ling)—a covering for the engine of an airplane or boat

drag (DRAYG)—something that makes action or progress slower or more difficult

horsepower (HORS-pow-uhr)—a unit used to measure the power of engines

hull (HUHL)—the main part of a ship or boat, including the deck, sides, and bottom

powerboat (PAH-wr-boht)—a boat with a motor that is meant for racing or going fast

sponson (SPAWN-sen)—a winglike part that comes off the hull of a seaplane or hydroplane to steady it on water

BOOKS

Gigliotti, Jim. *Powerboat Racing.* Mankato, MN: The Child's World, 2012.

Hauenstein, Michael. *Speedboat Racers.* Kid Racers. Berkeley Heights, NJ: Enslow Publishers, 2010.

MacArthur, Collin. *Inside a Speedboat.* Life in the Fast Lane. New York: Cavendish Square Publishing, 2015.

WEBSITES

American Power Boat Association
www.apba.org

GoPro: Fastest Hydroplane on Earth
www.youtube.com/watch?v=_AArltTNRaA

H1 Unlimited
www.h1unlimited.com

INDEX